Hawaii
The Aloha State

Marcia Amidon Lusted

PowerKiDS press™

New York

Published in 2011 by The Rosen Publishing Group, Inc.
29 East 21st Street, New York, NY 10010

First Edition

Editor: Maggie Murphy
Book Design: Greg Tucker
Layout Design: Kate Laczynski
Photo Researcher: Jessica Gerweck

Photo Credits: Cover, pp. 5, 7, 13, 19, 22 (tree, mammal, bird, flower) Shutterstock.com; p. 9 Art Wolfe/Getty Images; p. 11 Rich Reid/Getty Images; p. 15 © Frilet Patrick/age fotostock; p. 17 Holger Leue/Getty Images; p. 22 (Queen Liliuokalani) Hulton Archive/Getty Images; p. 22 (Barack Obama) Jewel Samad/AFP/Getty Images; p. 22 (Nicole Kidman) Christopher Polk/Getty Images.

Library of Congress Cataloging-in-Publication Data

Lusted, Marcia Amidon.
   Hawaii : the Aloha State / Marcia Amidon Lusted. — 1st ed.
      p. cm. — (Our amazing states)
   Includes index.
   ISBN 978-1-4488-0665-2 (library binding) — ISBN 978-1-4488-0766-6 (pbk.) —
ISBN 978-1-4488-0767-3 (6-pack)
   1. Hawaii—Juvenile literature. I. Title.
   DU623.25.L87 2011
   996.9—dc22
                                          2010000835

Manufactured in the United States of America

CPSIA Compliance Information: Batch #WS10PK: For Further Information contact Rosen Publishing, New York, New York at 1-800-237-9932

Contents

Welcome to the Islands

Which state is actually made up of eight islands, scattered across 1,500 miles (2,414 km) of the Pacific Ocean? Where can you find live **volcanoes** and see coral reefs? This state is located very far from any other places, but it is still part of the United States. It is also the country's newest state. Where are you? You are in Hawaii!

Hawaii is located 2,400 miles (3,862 km) southwest of California. It became the fiftieth state in 1959. With its warm **climate** and interesting history, Hawaii is very different from the other states.

Hawaii is nicknamed the Aloha State. *Aloha* is a Hawaiian word that means "hello" or "good-bye," as well as "love." Hawaiians use the word so often that the entire state is named for this friendly greeting.

This woman is doing a native Hawaiian dance, called hula. If you visit Hawaii, you will likely see a hula dance!

Kings, Queens, and Palaces

It is hard to imagine that a part of the United States had a royal palace. However, Hawaii was once ruled by King Kamehameha, who became king of the islands in 1795. Kings and queens ruled the Kingdom of Hawaii until it became a U.S. territory in 1900. They lived in the 'Iolani Palace, in what is now Honolulu.

King Kamehameha III, the grandson of the first king, created a **constitutional monarchy** in 1840. In 1848, he also made a new law called the Great Mahele, which gave land to some Hawaiian people for farming.

Hawaii's language was not written down until **missionaries** came to the islands in the 1820s. The Hawaiian language uses only 12 letters from the English alphabet, and something called the okina, which looks like a backward apostrophe.

The 'Iolani Palace, shown here, was built in 1882. Hawaii's last queen, Queen Liliuokalani, lived there when the Hawaiian monarchy was overthrown in 1893.

Land of Volcanoes

Hawaii's islands were created by a hot spot, or hole, on the ocean floor. Melted rock called magma escaped from Earth's core there and hardened when it met the cooler ocean water. This hardened rock created Hawaii's eight islands. Together the islands are an **archipelago**.

The state's biggest and southernmost island is called Hawaii, like the state. There you can find black sand beaches and some of the state's biggest volcanoes. The Kilauea volcano is still erupting, and its lava adds new land to the island every year.

North of Hawaii is the island of Maui. There, the East Maui volcano, a **dormant** volcano, rises 10,000 feet (3,048 m) above the ocean. Its ancient crater, known as Haleakala Crater, is filled with colorful rocks.

Here you can see lava flows from the erupting Kilauea volcano, on the island of Hawaii. Some Hawaiians believe Kilauea is the home of Pele, the Hawaiian Volcano goddess.

Island-Hopping

As you move north, you will find Kahoolawe, Lanai, and Molokai. No one lives on Kahoolawe, the smallest Hawaiian island, but many sheep and cattle once fed on its gentle **slopes**. On Lanai, there are beaches as well as the high top of Lana'ihale. Molokai is known for its high waterfalls and steep sea cliffs.

Moving north again, you will find the island of Oahu, which is home to Pearl Harbor and many sandy beaches. Above Oahu is the island of Kauai, where you will find steep cliffs and the Waimea Canyon. Hawaii's northernmost island is Niihau, where sheep and cattle are raised on ranches.

Hawaii's climate is usually warm, except on the highest mountaintops, where it sometimes snows. Some of the islands receive more rain than the others.

This is a rocky beach on the western shore of Molokai. The forests on the eastern side of the island can get as much as 300 inches (760 cm) of rain each year.

Pineapples and Wild Horses

Many of the fruits and grasses found on Hawaii, such as pineapples, papayas, bananas, sugarcane, and mangoes, are grown to be sold in stores and markets. The macadamia nuts and coffee beans you see in the store may have also come from Hawaii!

Wildflowers, such as red ginger and blue jade vine, grow on the islands. These flowers are shaded by magnolia, candlenut, and koa trees. Coconut trees dot the shores of Kauai.

Hawaii's animals include **mongooses**, deer, wild goats, and donkeys. On the big island of Hawaii, wild horses wander through the Waipi'o Valley. Monk seals come to the beaches of Kauai to give birth to their pups. The state mammal is the humpback whale, which swims in the ocean around Maui.

Many people think the pineapple comes from Hawaii. Actually, the fruit is native to South America. Pineapples were first grown in Hawaii in the early 1800s.

What Do People Do in Hawaii?

Many people in Hawaii work in jobs that provide food, housing, and entertainment for **tourists**. Others work on military bases. Because of its location in the middle of the Pacific Ocean, the Army, Navy, Air Force, and Marines all have bases there.

Hawaii is famous for growing pineapples, macadamia nuts, and coffee. Some of the flowers you can find for sale in other states may have been grown there as well. Fishermen bring in swordfish and bigeye tuna. Factories **process** some of Hawaii's crops, turning sugarcane into sugar and canning pineapples. Coffee beans are roasted and packed for sale.

Hawaiian cowboys, called *paniolos*, herd cattle on ranches on the island of Hawaii. The cows are then sent by ship to the mainland.

This paniolo works in the Waimea area, on the island of Hawaii. The skills of paniolos are celebrated at the Paniolo Parade in Waimea, held each year during the Hawaii Island Festival.

City of Royalty

Hawaii's capital city, Honolulu, was once home to its kings and queens. The 'Iolani Palace still stands, and at one point it was used as Hawaii's statehouse. In Honolulu you can also visit the Chinatown area with its markets and restaurants. Then take a drive to the Nuuanu Pali lookout, where you can see the Koolau Range.

Near Honolulu is Waikiki Beach, where visitors and locals surf and swim. You can also wander through a maze at the Dole Pineapple Plantation or hike through the rain forests and see some of Oahu's **sacred** places. Are you hungry? Then enjoy pork cooked in an underground oven at a luau, or native Hawaiian feast. Are you ready for dessert? Try some coconut pudding or fresh pineapple!

Here, a surfer carries his surfboard toward the water at Waikiki Beach. There is a statue of Duke Kahanamoku, who made modern surfing a popular sport, there.

Visit a Volcano

If you visit the Hawaii Volcanoes National Park, on the island of Hawaii, you will have the chance to see active volcanoes. Both Kilauea and Mauna Loa still erupt, and visitors to the park can see **cinder cones**, flowing lava, and fountains of lava splatter. Ash and smoke rise from fresh holes in the volcanoes and where lava flows into the ocean.

The park is also home to many plants that grow only in Hawaii. The rare silversword plant, which Hawaiians call *ahinahina*, grows up high on the volcanoes. Giant hapuu, a kind of Hawaiian fern, grows in the rain forest, while a'e ferns grow from holes in the lava flows. Many of these plants are now **endangered** species.

You can see many lava forms at Hawaii Volcanoes National Park. This bright orange spot is called a lava skylight. A lava skylight is a hole in the roof of an underground pool of lava.

Come to Hawaii!

People from all over the world know that Hawaii is a wonderful place to visit. Visitors to the islands often receive a kiss of welcome from locals and a beautiful lei, which is a **garland** of flowers.

You can see Polynesian boats and watch men and women hula dance. You can also visit the rain forest and mountains and watch sharks and green sea turtles in the Pacific Ocean. You can take a helicopter **tour** of the islands and their beautiful scenery. You can surf in the waves off one of Hawaii's many beaches, too.

No matter what you like to do, Hawaii has something you will love. Maybe that is one of the reasons why it is called the Aloha State!

Glossary

archipelago (ar-kih-PEH-luh-goh) A group of islands.

cinder cones (SIN-der KOHNZ) Cone-shaped hills of rock pieces around volcanoes.

climate (KLY-mit) The kind of weather a certain area has.

constitutional monarchy (kon-stih-TOO-shuh-nul MAH-nar-kee) A government in which a country has both a ruler and elected leaders.

dormant (DOR-ment) Resting, not active.

endangered (in-DAYN-jerd) In danger of no longer existing.

garland (GAR-land) A circle of flowers or leaves.

missionaries (MIH-shuh-ner-eez) People sent to another country to tell people about a certain faith.

mongooses (MON-goos-ez) Weasel-like animals that can kill poisonous snakes.

process (PRAH-ses) To treat or change something using a special series of steps.

sacred (SAY-kred) Highly respected and considered very important.

slopes (SLOHPS) Hills.

tour (TOUR) A trip on which many places are visited.

tourists (TUR-ists) People visiting a place where they do not live.

volcanoes (vol-KAY-nohz) Openings in the surface of Earth that sometimes shoot up a hot liquid rock called lava.

Hawaii State Symbols

State Tree
Candlenut Tree

State Mammal
Humpback
Whale

State Flag

State Bird
Nene

State Flower
Hawaiian
Hibiscus

State Seal

Famous People from Hawaii

Queen Liliuokalani
(1838–1917)
Born in Honolulu, HI
Last Monarch of the
Kingdom of Hawaii

Barack Obama
(1961–)
Born in Honolulu, HI
U.S. President

Nicole Kidman
(1967–)
Born in Honolulu, HI
Actress

Hawaii State Map

KAUAI

NIIHAU

OAHU

Pearl Harbor ★ **Honolulu**

MOLOKAI

Kahului

Lanai City

LANAI

MAUI

East Maui Volcano

KAHOOLAWE

Legend

○ Major City

★ Capital

〜 *River*

Mauna Loa

Hilo

HAWAII

Hawaii State Facts

Population: About 1,211,537

Area: 10,931 square miles (28,311 sq km)

Motto: "The Life of the Land Is Perpetuated in Righteousness"

Song: "Hawaii's Own," words by King David Kalakaua and music by Henry Berger

Index

C
climate, 4, 10

G
garland, 20
Great Mahele, 6

H
history, 4
Honolulu, Hawaii,
    6, 16

K
Kamehameha, King, 6
Kamehameha III
    (king), 6

L
language, 6
law, 6

M
maze, 16
missionaries, 6
mongooses, 12

O
ocean, 4, 8, 12, 14, 18

P
palace, 6, 16
people, 6, 14, 20
plants, 18

Q
queens, 6, 16

R
rock, 8

S
slopes, 10

T
territory, 6
tour, 20
tourists, 14

V
volcanoes, 4, 8, 18

Web Sites

Due to the changing nature of Internet links, PowerKids Press has developed an online list of Web sites related to the subject of this book. This site is updated regularly. Please use this link to access the list:
www.powerkidslinks.com/amst/hi/

24